Rigby On Our Way to English

Language Learning Masters

Grade 1

Welcome Centre

**with
Newcomer Masters
Handwriting Masters**

Contents

On Our Way to English

Using the Language Learning Masters

These blackline masters support instruction in the *On Our Way to English* Thematic Teacher's Guide. Each unit is comprised of a Manipulative Chart Student Version, a set of TPR Cards, a Language Practice Game, and three Grammar Masters.

- **Manipulative Chart Student Versions**
  These smaller versions of the Manipulative Charts allow for individual interaction with the Manipulative Chart chants. Children can take the student versions home for sharing with family members. When laminated, student versions can be revisited countless times in a Language Center. Teacher assistance is required during assembly.

- **TPR Cards—Total Physical Response**
  Each set of twelve TPR Cards reviews and introduces additional vocabulary through Total Physical Response. They can be used for interactive whole-class participation or individual review. TPR Card sets are sometimes used for playing the Language Practice Game.

- **Language Practice Games**
  Language Practice Games provide multiple opportunities for language practice in a meaningful context. The game atmosphere encourages learning through cooperation. Although assembly is required, games can be saved from one year to the next. Full instructions for assembly and game directions are in the *On Our Way to English* Thematic Teacher's Guide.

- **Grammar Masters**
  The Grammar Masters provide children practice with grammar points learned during the unit. Each Grammar Master is leveled according to the five stages of language acquisition. These masters can also be used for assessment and can be included in children's portfolios.

Newcomer Activity Masters

Newcomer Activity Masters introduce English language learners at the beginning stages of language acquisition to everyday language. These masters can be used with any unit based on teacher observation of children's progress.

Handwriting Masters

Handwriting Masters provide practice with letter formation for the entire alphabet. Directions for the teacher are provided for each master.

On Our Way to English

Get your **backpack** ready
Get your **backpack** ready
Get your **backpack** ready
Because it is time for school.

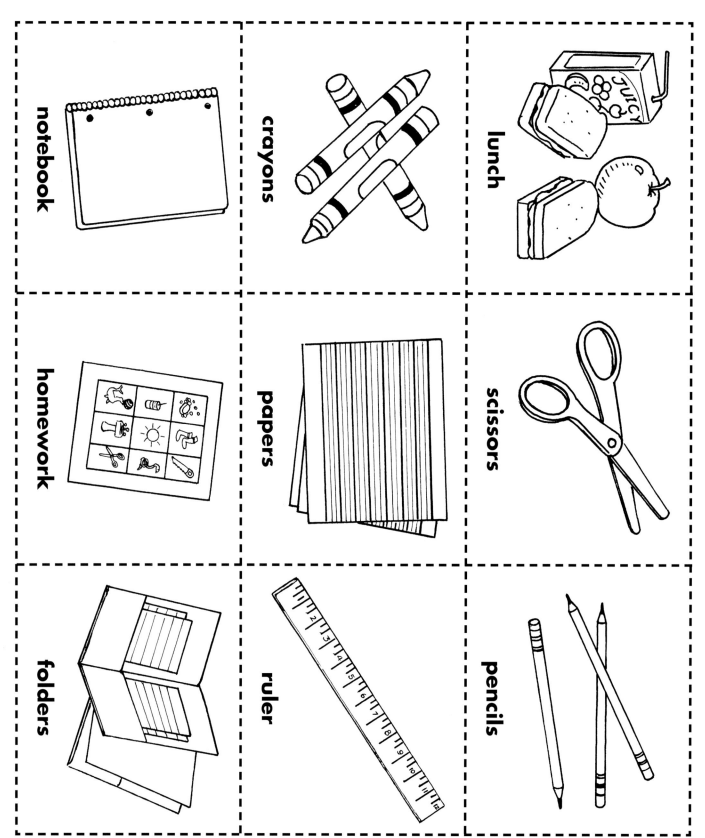

notebook

crayons

lunch

homework

papers

scissors

folders

ruler

pencils

Directions: Cut out the pictures along the dotted lines. Place each picture on the backpack on page 5.

desk

chair

pencils

crayons

paper

ruler

books

apple

sandwich

cookies

carrot

juice

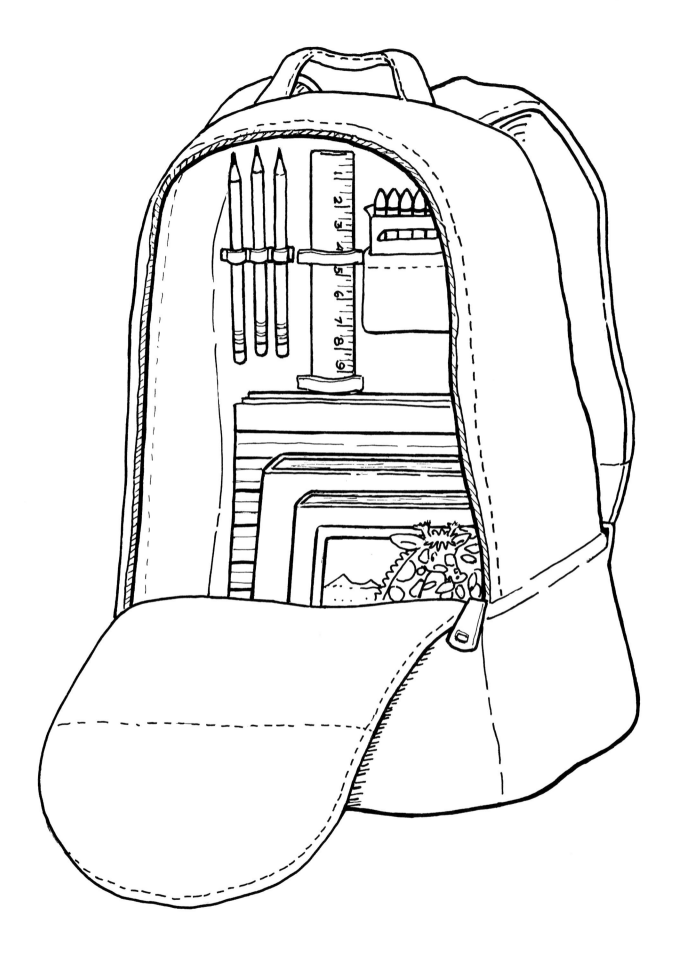

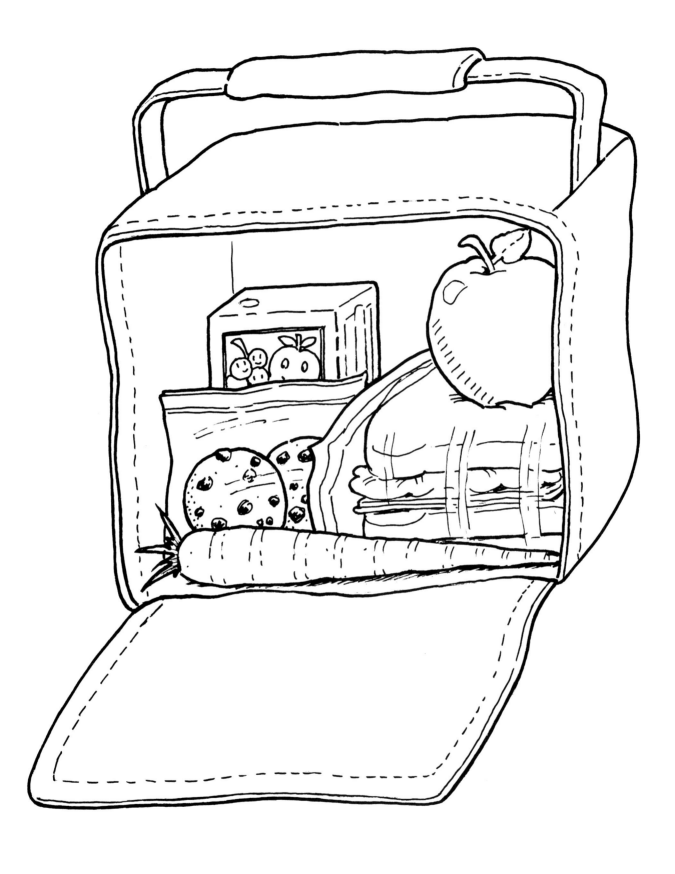

Things I Do at School

Look at the picture.
What is the child doing?
Write the word.

cut 	draw	read	write

1. I _____ at school.

2. I _____ at school.

3. I _____ at school.

4. I _____ at school.

Directions: Have children complete each sentence with the word that matches each picture. You may want to save this page in children's portfolios.

Name_____

School Fun

Look at the picture.
Write **He** or **She**.

_____
- - - - - - - - - - - - - -
1. _____ likes to read.

_____
- - - - - - - - - - - - - -
2. _____ likes to jump.

_____
- - - - - - - - - - - - - -
3. _____ likes to draw.

_____
- - - - - - - - - - - - - -
4. _____ likes to write.

Directions: Have children look at the picture and choose the pronoun that completes the sentence.

Unit 1   Subject Pronouns: *he, she*   STAGES ①②❸❹❺   **11**

Name_____

Ready to Work

How many things do they need?
Match each card to a picture.

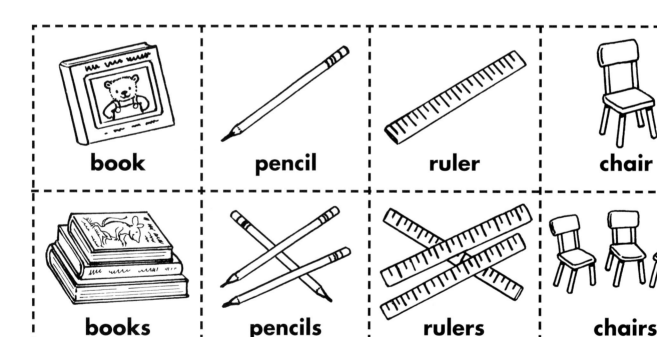

book	**pencil**	**ruler**	**chair**
books	**pencils**	**rulers**	**chairs**

Directions: Have children cut out the cards. Ask questions such as *Which table needs three chairs?*
Have children match the number of items on the card with the picture that has the same number of
people. You may want to save this page in children's portfolios.

How do you use your **ears**?
How do you use your **ears**?
Oh, won't you tell me now?
How do you use your **ears**?

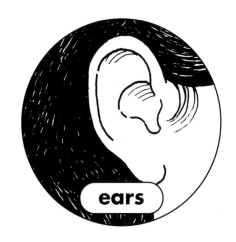

ears

nose

mouth

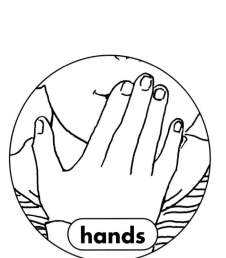

hands

eyes

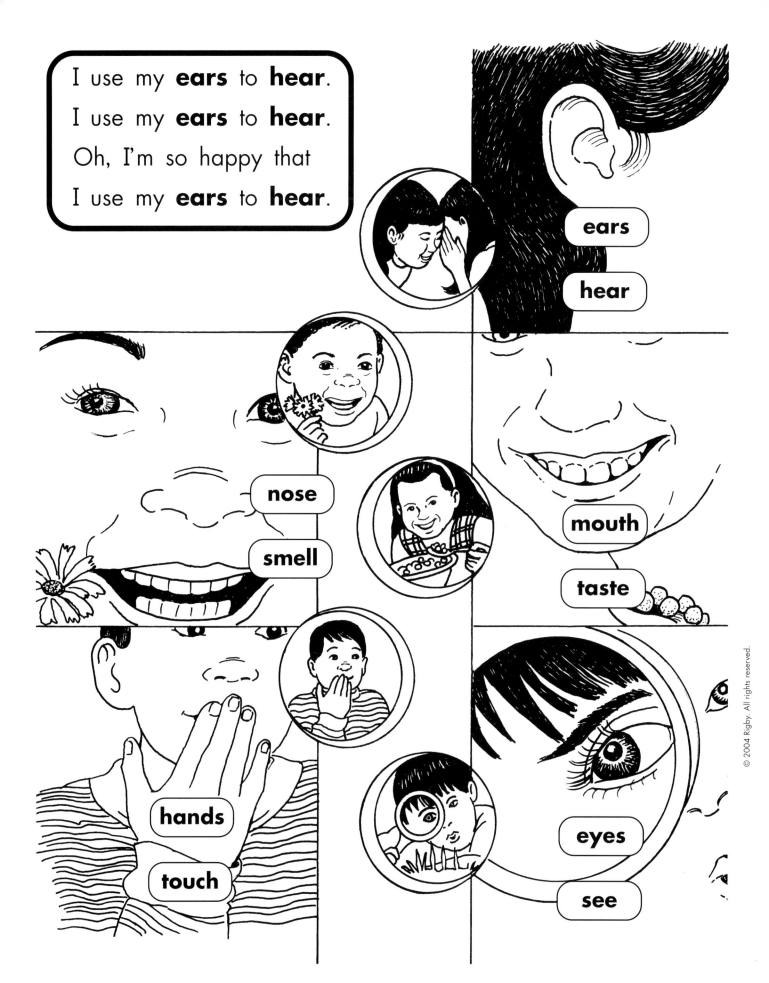

I use my **ears** to **hear**.
I use my **ears** to **hear**.
Oh, I'm so happy that
I use my **ears** to **hear**.

ears

hear

nose

smell

mouth

taste

hands

touch

eyes

see

Directions: Tape page 13 on top of page 14 along the left-hand side.

taste

feel

see

smell

hear

father

grandpa

mother

grandma

sister

brother

family

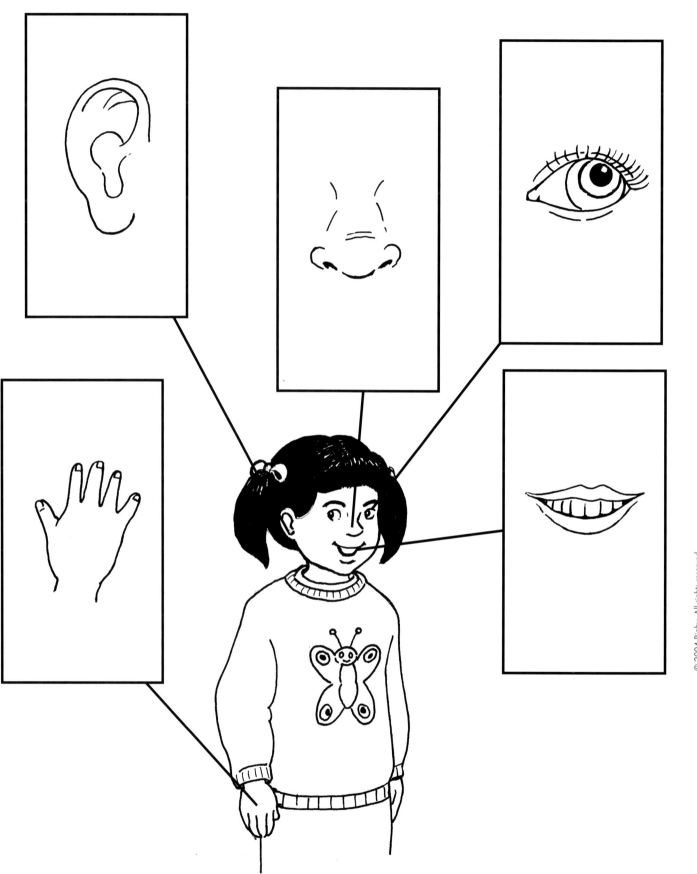

Language Practice Game

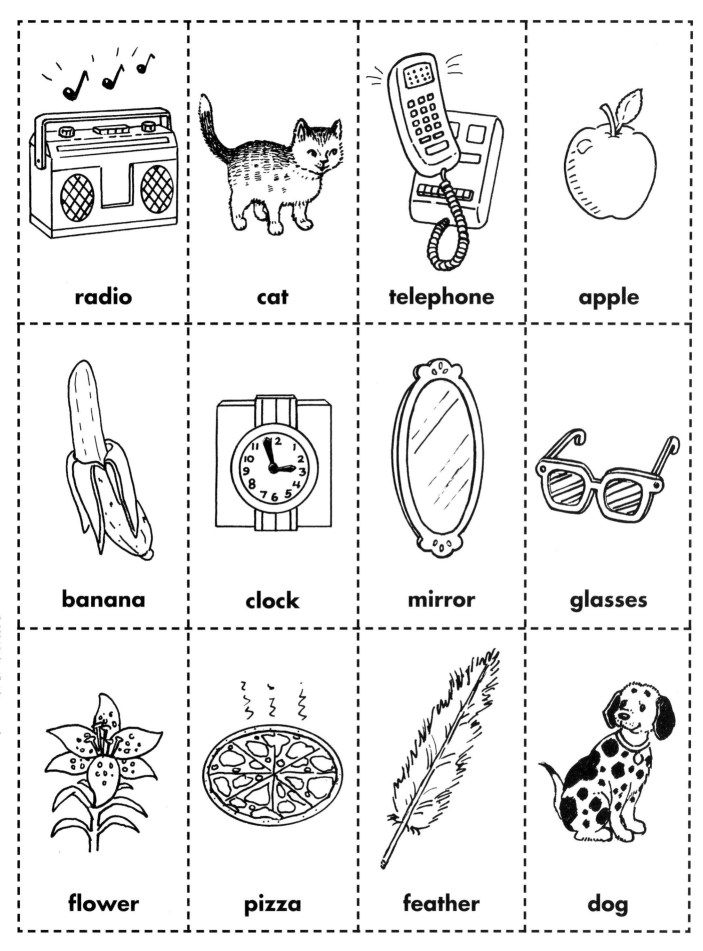

radio	**cat**	**telephone**	**apple**
banana	**clock**	**mirror**	**glasses**
flower	**pizza**	**feather**	**dog**

Name_____

Favorite Colors

Ask some friends *What is your favorite color?*
Color a box for each answer.

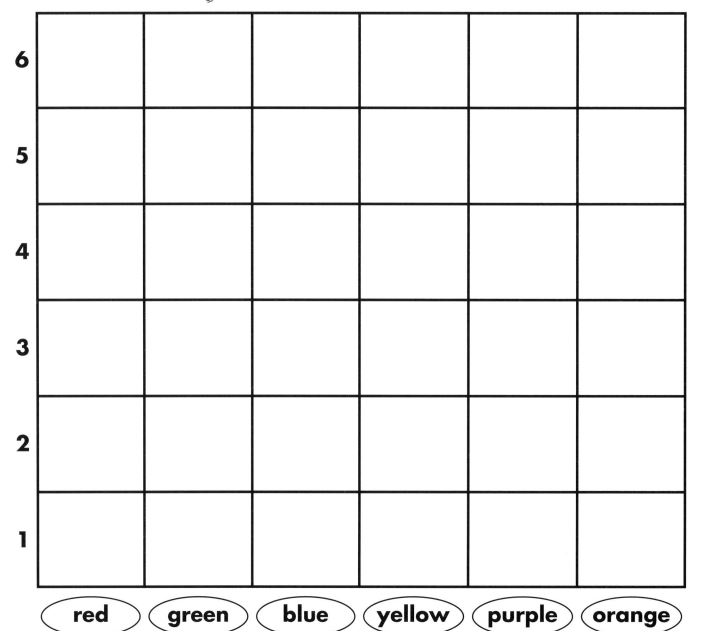

Directions: Have children color the ovals the appropriate colors. Then invite children to ask classmates *What is your favorite color?* Children color in the appropriate box in the graph according to classmates' responses. You may want to save this page in children's portfolios.

Name_____

It or They?

Listen to your teacher.
Circle the correct picture for each sentence.

1. It is a house.

2. It is a cat.

3. They are hands.

4. It is a dog.

5. They are girls.

6. They are boys.

Directions: Have children circle the subject pronoun for each sentence. Ask them to circle the picture that matches the subject pronoun.

Who Is in the Kitchen?

Listen to your teacher.

Directions: Read the following questions to children, pausing between each one. Say *Who is smelling the flowers? Who is eating an apple? Who is reading? Who is playing with a rattle? Who is making dinner?* Invite the children to circle the correct person. You may want to save this page in children's portfolios.

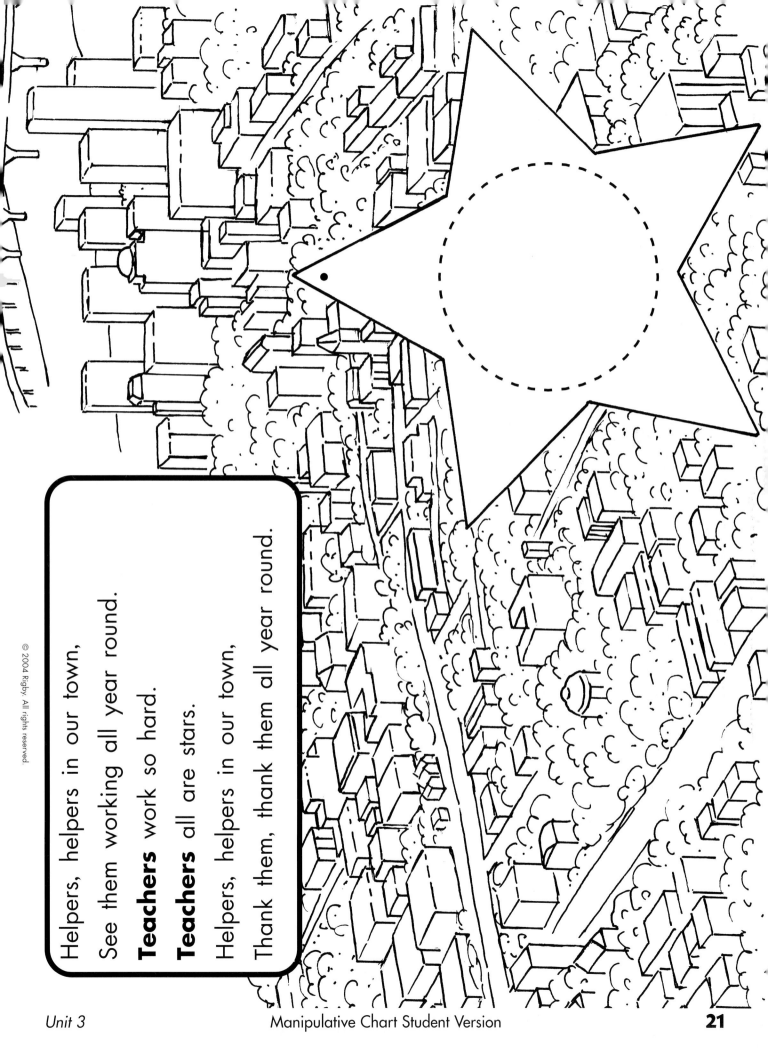

Helpers, helpers in our town,
See them working all year round.
Teachers work so hard.
Teachers all are stars.

Helpers, helpers in our town,
Thank them, thank them all year round.

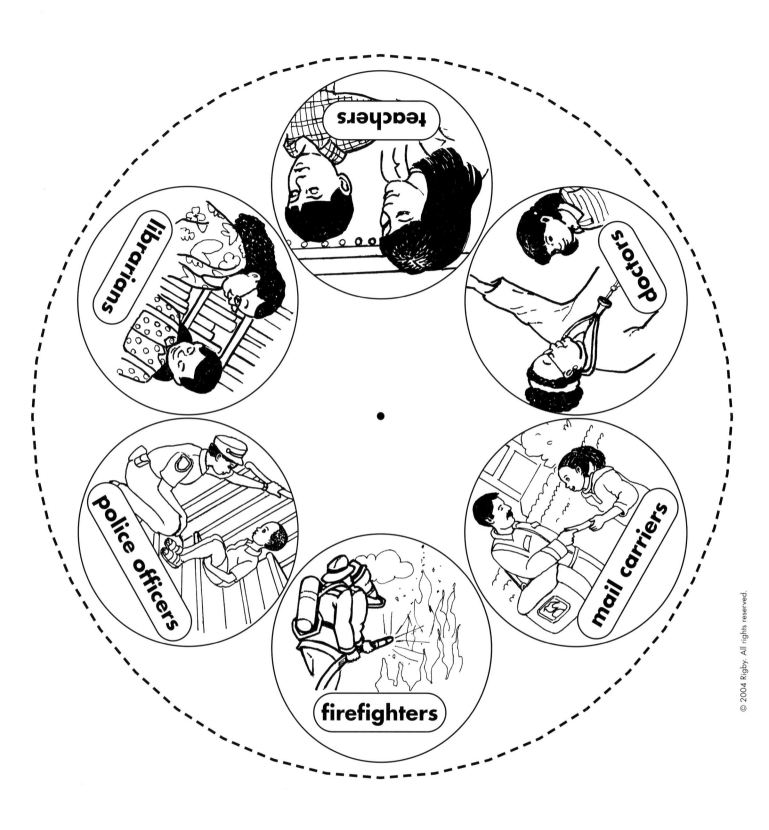

Directions: Cut out the hole on page 21. Cut out the wheel on page 22. Line up the wheel behind page 21 so that you can see the pictures through the hole. Use a fastener to secure.

mail carrier	teacher	firefighter	librarian
baker	bus driver	doctor	post office
school	fire station	library	bakery

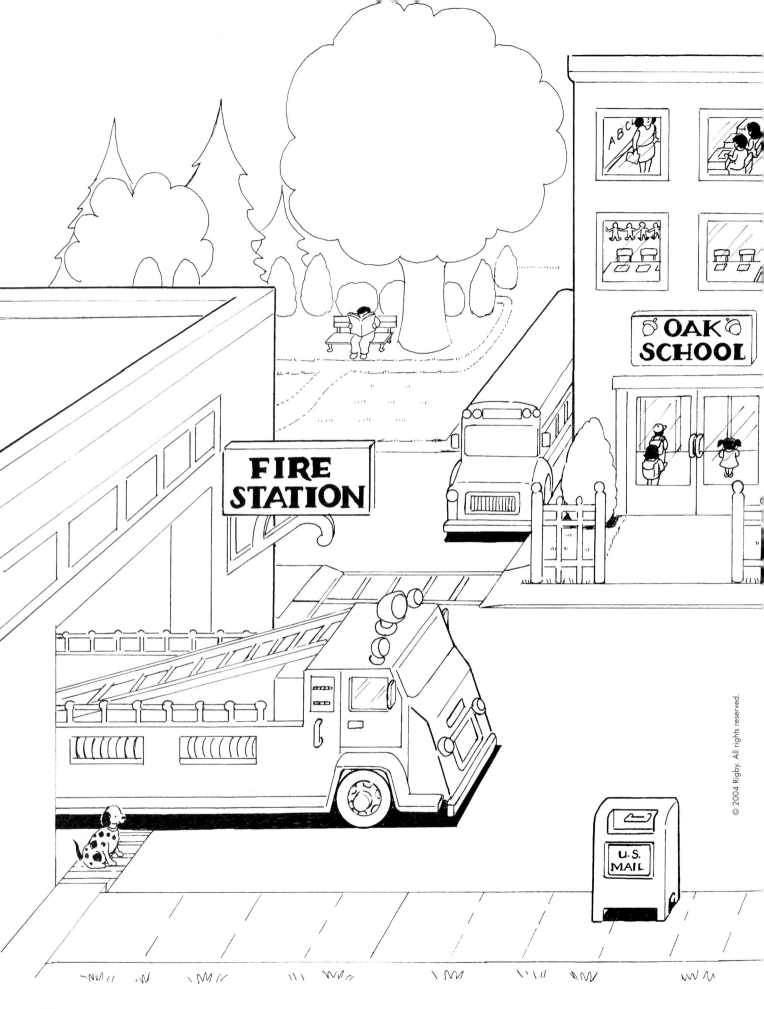

FIRE STATION

OAK SCHOOL

U.S. MAIL

BAKERY

LIBRARY

Unit 3   Language Practice Game   **25**

Name_____

Workers in Our Town

Look at the pictures.
Write **is** or **is not**.

_____
- -
1. She _____ a teacher.
_____
- -
She _____ a firefighter.

_____
- -
2. He _____ a police officer.
_____
- -
He _____ a mail carrier.

_____
- -
3. She _____ a baker.
_____
- -
She _____ a doctor.

Directions: Have children look at each picture and write **is** or **is not** to tell about the picture.

Negative sentences with *is* (STAGES ①②❸❹❺) *Unit 3*

Name_____

In My Home

Draw something in your home.

_____

- -

My _____ is in my home.

Directions: Have children draw a picture of something in their home. Have them complete the sentence as they are able. You may want to save this page in children's portfolios.

What Did Carmen Do?

Listen to your teacher.
Match the sentence with the picture.

Carmen went to school yesterday. This is what she did.

1. She walked.

2. She played.

3. She laughed.

4. She painted.

Directions: Read the sentences aloud to children. Have children draw a line from the sentence to the picture that matches. You may want to save this page in children's portfolios.

rainy

Do you like it when it's **rainy**?

What do you wear then?

Do you like it when it's **rainy**?

Can you play outside with friends?

Do you like it when it's **rainy**?

What you wear and do will change

When the weather changes again.

hot

cool

Directions: Cut out the pictures on this page along the dotted lines. Place them on top of each other. Staple them to page 29 along the left-hand side.

sunny

Do you like it when it's **sunny**?

What do you wear then?

Do you like it when it's **sunny**?

Can you play outside with friends?

Do you like it when it's **sunny**?

What you wear and do will change

When the weather changes again.

snowy

windy

Directions: Cut out the pictures on this page along the dotted lines. Place them on top of each other. Staple them to page 31 along the left-hand side.

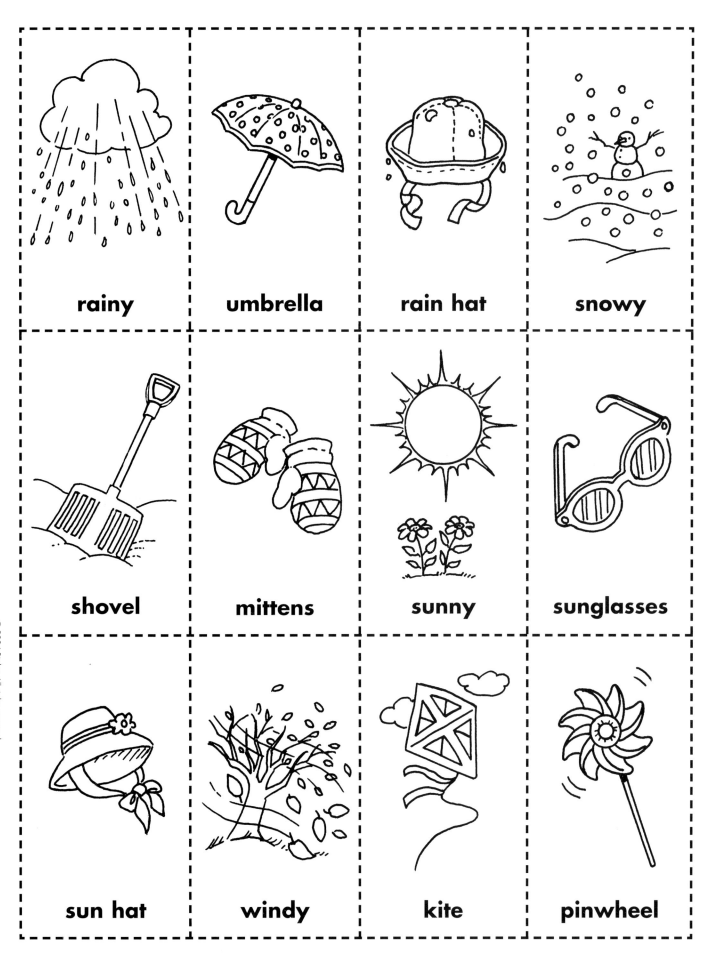

rainy	**umbrella**	**rain hat**	**snowy**
shovel	**mittens**	**sunny**	**sunglasses**
sun hat	**windy**	**kite**	**pinwheel**

Board 1

windy	sunglasses
umbrella	snowy
sunny	kite

Board 2

pinwheel	rainy
sunny	shovel
rain hat	windy

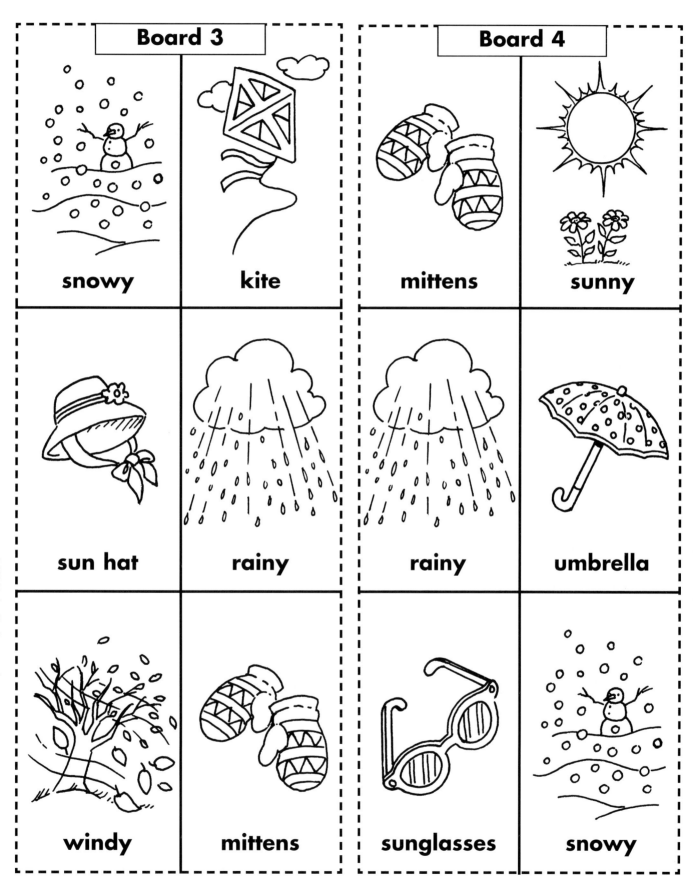

Board 3

snowy	**kite**
sun hat	**rainy**
windy	**mittens**

Board 4

mittens	**sunny**
rainy	**umbrella**
sunglasses	**snowy**

Name_____

What Time Is It?

Write I's on the line.
Read the sentence.

1. _____ 7 o'clock.

2. _____ 8 o'clock.

3. _____ 12 o'clock.

4. _____ 3 o'clock.

Directions: Have children write the contraction *It's* on the line to complete the sentence.

Contractions with *is* STAGES ①②③④⑤   Unit 4

Name_____

What Is Happening?

Read the sentence.
Look at the picture.
Write the word.

1. It is _____ .

    raining   snowing

2. It is _____ .

    raining   snowing

3. The boy is _____ .

       reading   jumping

4. The baby is _____ .

       jumping   crying

Directions: Have children look at the pictures and write the correct word for each sentence. Children can circle the word as well. You may want to save this page in children's portfolios.

Name_____

How Big and How Small?

Draw pictures to match the words.

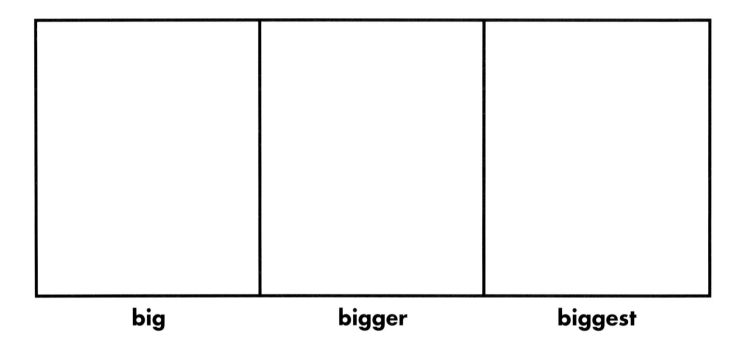

| big | bigger | biggest |

| small | smaller | smallest |

Directions: Have children look at each group of words. Help children read the words. Find examples in the classroom that demonstrate comparisons. Then have children draw a picture in each box to show the comparison. You may want to save this page in children's portfolios.

Animals all have special homes,
Hurrah, hurrah!
Animals all have special homes,
Hurrah, hurrah!
What about **birds**?
Their home is a **nest**.
Birds live in a **nest**.
Birds sleep in a **nest**.
And **birds** care for their babies
in a **nest**!

Directions: Cut along two slits on page 39. Cut out the two strips above. Feed strips up through right slit and down through left so that pictures are visible.

duck	**duckling**	**mouse**	**sheep**
bear	**bee**	**bat**	**bird**
cat	**goose**	**fish**	**squirrel**

Name_____

Animal Puzzles

Match the puzzle pieces.

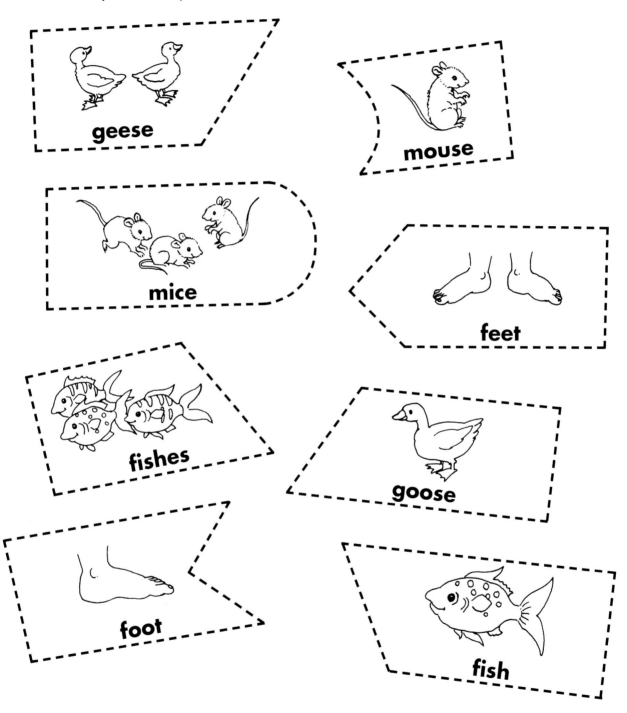

geese

mouse

mice

feet

fishes

goose

foot

fish

Directions: Have children cut out the puzzle pieces and match the singular and plural forms of the nouns. Ask children to say the singular and plural nouns.

Name_____

Monkey and Friends

Listen to your teacher.
Color the animals.

Directions: Have children color the animal. 1.The bee on top of the monkey red; 2.The bird in the monkey's hand blue; 3.The lizard behind the monkey yellow; 4.The bat next to the monkey green; 5.The bird under the monkey purple; 6.The bird on the monkey's foot orange. You may want to save this page in the children's portfolios.

Animal Homes

Read each sentence.
Write the correct word or words.

_____

_____ in a house.

ve   lives

_____

_____ in a pond.

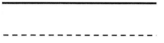
iive   lives

_____

3. Bears _____ in a den.

live   lives

4. A cow _____ in a house.

lives   does not live

5. A bird _____ in a den.

lives   does not live

Directions: Have children write the correct word or words on the line. They may also circle the word. You may want to save this page in children's portfolios.

Babies grow older every day.
Babies grow older every day.
Babies need **diapers**
And **babies** need **families**.
They will need these things
to grow and to change.

Directions: Cut out the cards on this page to lay on top of page 47.

seed	**tree**	**puppy**	**dog**
kitten	**cat**	**chick**	**chicken**
babies	**children**	**dads**	**grandpas**

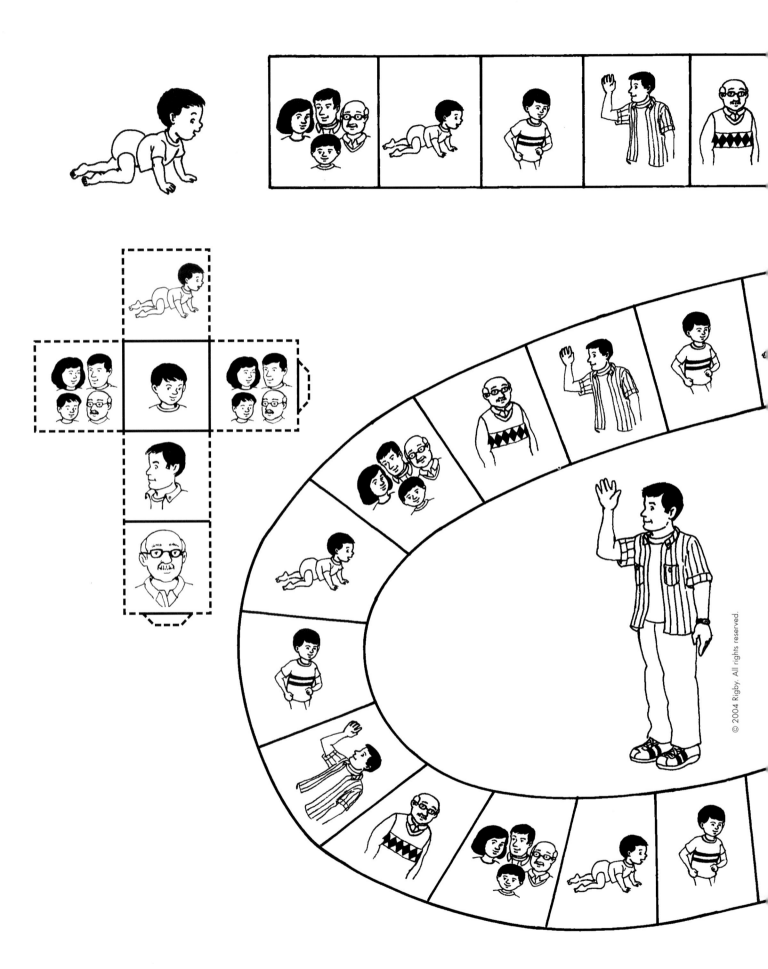

Language Practice Game

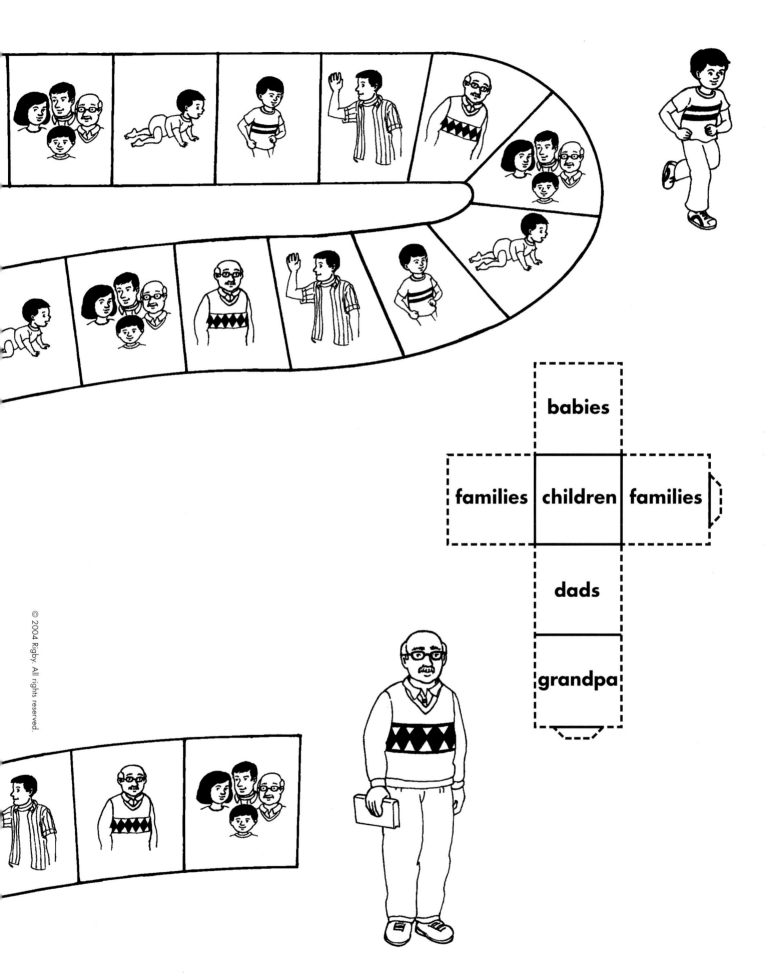

babies

families | children | families

dads

grandpa

Name_____

In the Garden

Look at the picture.
Write **There is** or **There are** in each sentence.

_____
- -

1. _____ seeds in the garden.

_____
- -

2. _____ a bird in the garden.

_____
- -

3. _____ a girl in the garden.

_____
- -

4. _____ flowers in the garden.

Directions: Have children decide if the sentence refers to singular or plural nouns and write *There is* or *There are* to complete each sentence. You may discuss other items in the garden. You may want to save this in children's portfolios.

Name_____

How Did She Grow?

Cut the pictures.
Paste them in order.

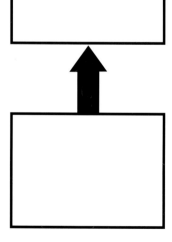

The teenager grew into a woman.

The girl grew into a teenager.

The baby grew into a girl.

A baby was born.

Directions: Have children cut out the pictures and paste them in the appropriate box. Then read the sentences to the children. Invite children to answer the question *How did she grow?*

I Will Be Big

Cut out the cards.
Match the beginning and end of each sentence.

Directions: Have children cut out the puzzle pieces and match the beginning and end of each sentence. Stages 1 and 2 can match the pictures and practice saying each animal's name. Encourage Stages 3–5 to say the complete sentences. You may want to save this page in children's portfolios.

To keep me feeling healthy,
I need **food** and **water**
Every day, every day.

What do I need
What do I need
Every day, every day?

Manipulative Chart Student Version

play

exercise

soap

toothpaste

sleep

rest

food

water

clothes

shoes

Directions: Cut out the pictures on this page. Place them on the windows on page 55.

water

shoes

clothes

soap

bath

toothbrush

seat belt

helmet

knee pads

stop

traffic light

smoke detector

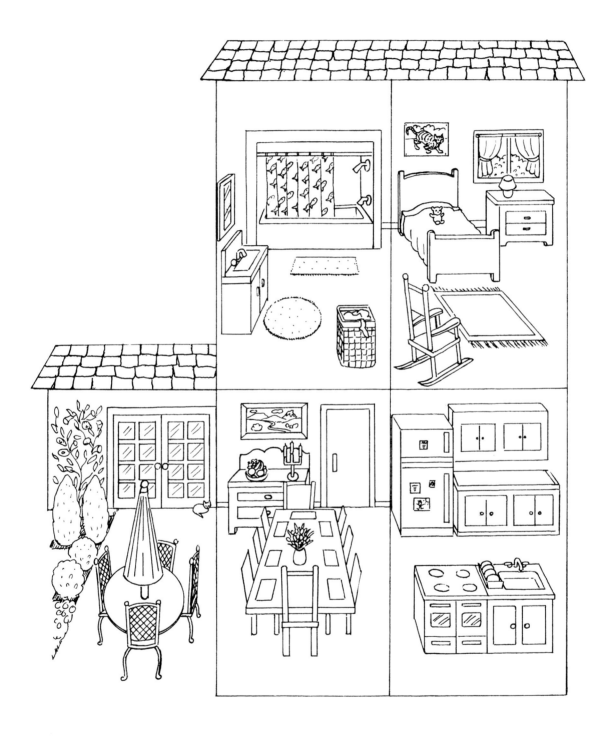

play	**shampoo**	**soap**	**toothpaste**
brush	**comb**	**sleep**	**clothes**
shoes	**food**	**water**	**love**

Name_____

Where Are They?

Cut and fold.
Ask your friends questions.

1. Where is the girl playing?

2. Where is the girl sleeping?

3. Where is the boy eating?

4. Where is the boy washing his hands?

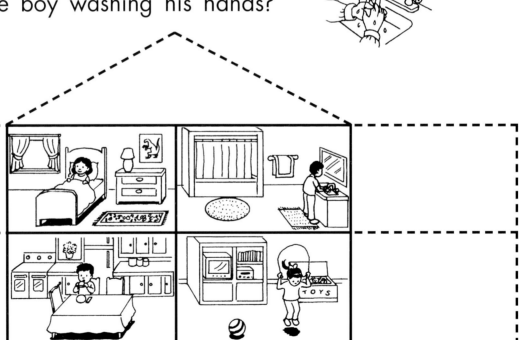

Directions: Have children cut along dotted lines, stopping where the house begins. Fold along left and right sides of house to make flaps to cover rooms. Have children ask and answer the questions by pointing, gesturing, approximating, or saying a sentence, as they are able.

Name_____

Things I Do

Read each sentence.
Write **because** on the line.

1. I go to  _____ I am  .

2. I use an  _____ it is  .

3. I wear a  _____ I am  .

4. I take a  _____ I am  .

Directions: Read each rebus sentence. Then have children write the word **because** on the line. You may want to save this page in children's portfolios.

You Can Do It

Tell your partner what to do.

Brush your teeth.

Jump rope.

Wash your hands.

Eat an apple.

Hop up and down.

Tie your shoes.

Directions: Have children work in pairs and take turns giving each other commands to act out. Children may color in the pictures when they have completed all the actions. Children in Stages 1 and 2 can follow the commands. You may want to save this page in the children's portfolios.

Can you find the **highest mountain**
Can you find the **highest mountain**
Can you find the **highest mountain**
On our big round Earth?

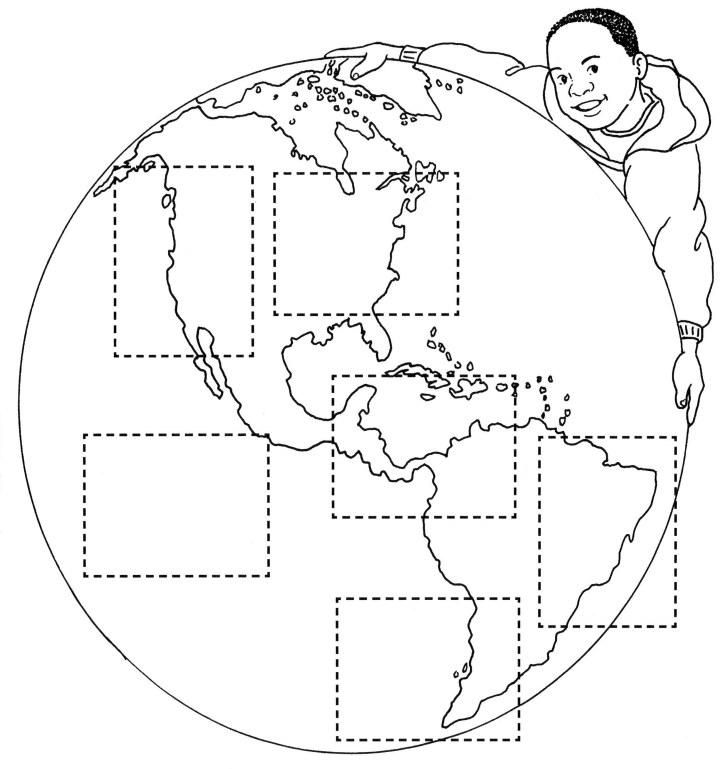

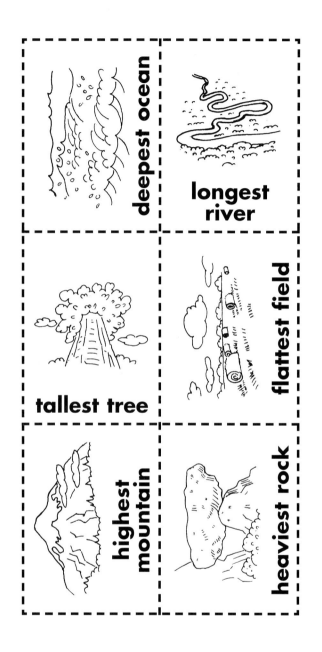

Directions: Cut out the pictures on this page. Match the pictures to the squares on page 63.

Manipulative Chart Student Version

tree	**river**	**mountain**	**flower**
rock	**lake**	**hill**	**field**
desert	**forest**	**island**	**Earth**

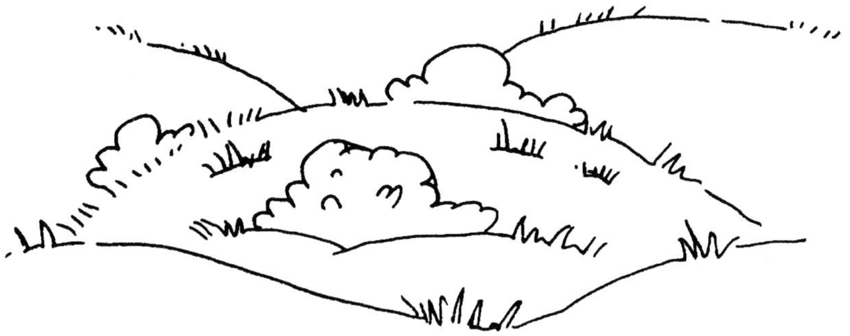

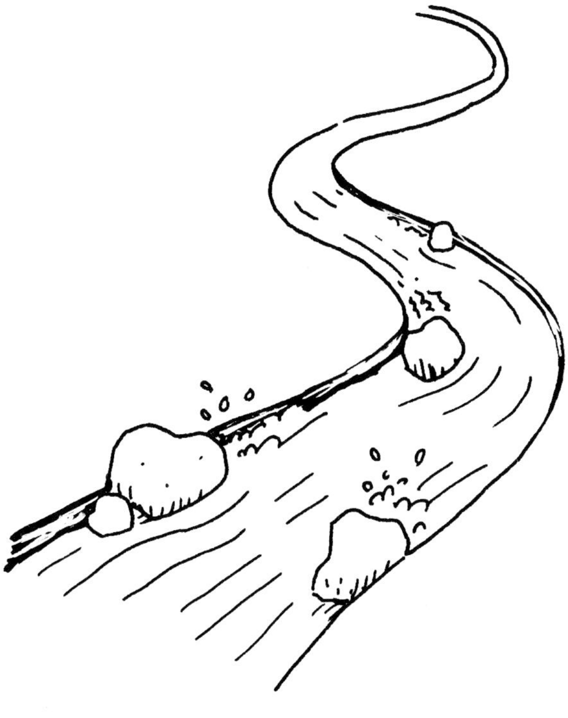

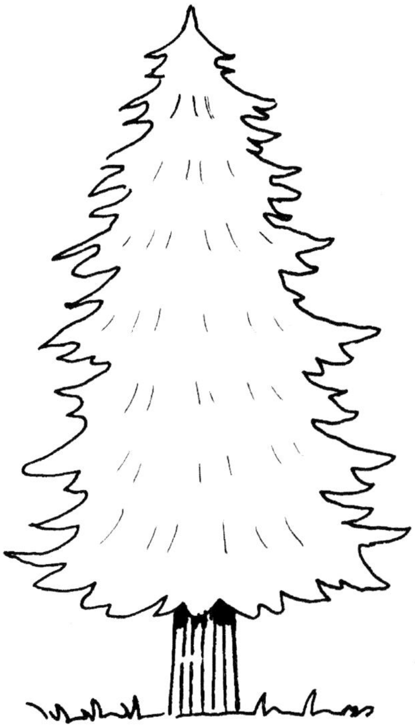

Name_____

How Many?

Use the graph.
Write the number.

1. How many ? _____
   _ _ _ _ _ _ _ _
   _____

2. How many ? _____
   _ _ _ _ _ _ _ _
   _____

3. How many more than ? _____ more
   _ _ _ _ _ _ _ _

4. How many fewer than ? _____ fewer
   _ _ _ _ _ _ _ _

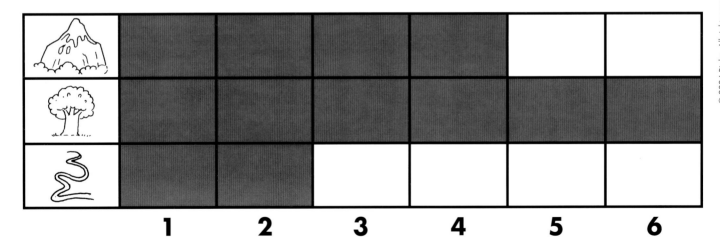

Directions: Have children use the graph to answer the questions. Discuss fewest and most by looking at the graph and the answers to questions 1–4. Have children circle the number that shows the most and put a triangle around the number that shows the fewest. You may want to save this page in children's portfolios.

Name_____

What Do You Do?

Work with a partner.
Circle the answers.

_____
- -

My Partner's Name _____

1. Do you swim?

I swim.

I don't swim.

2. Do you cook?

I cook.

I don't cook.

3. Do you drive?

I drive.

I don't drive.

4. Do you clean?

I clean.

I don't clean.

Directions: Have children ask a partner questions. The partner who responds writes his or her name on the line. Children should circle responses to the questions. Continue by prompting children with questions like *Does Luis draw?*

Unit 8   Negative sentences with do/does (STAGES ❶❷❸❹❺)   **69**

Name_____

Look Around

Read each word.
Draw a picture for each word.

small	**round**
long	**tall**
big	**flat**

Directions: Have children read each word and look around the room. Invite them to draw an object in each box that matches the word. You may want to save this page in children's portfolios.

Newcomer Activity
Masters

▲▲▲▲▲▲▲

Handwriting
Masters

Greeting Friends

Listen to your teacher.

Goodnight

Goodbye

Hello

Directions: Encourage children to act out what they see in the pictures. Then have them draw a line from the picture to the correct greeting. Children can say each greeting, as they are able.

⭐ **Extend:** Ask children to think of places outside of school where they might greet others. Then have them draw a picture of themselves in one of the places and write their greeting.

Let's Be Friends

Draw yourself with others.

"Hi. My name is Ana."

"Hello Ana. My name is Marco."

Directions: Have children draw a picture of themselves greeting classmates in different situations at school. Then encourage them to say the greetings above, as they are able.

⭐ **Extend:** Encourage children to say the greetings in their home language to one another.

Introductions, Greetings, and Names

73

Name_____

Count How Many

Color. Count.

Write the number.

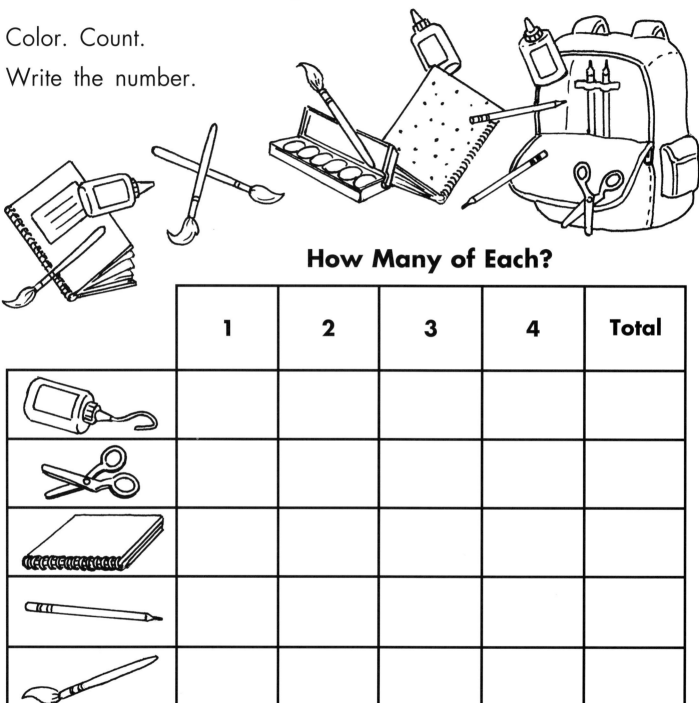

How Many of Each?

	1	2	3	4	Total
(glue)					
(scissors)					
(notebook)					
(pencil)					
(paintbrush)					

Directions: Show children how to color one box on the graph for each backpack item shown. They may want to cross out items as they record them. When they finish, ask them to count the boxes for each item and write the number, as they are able.

⭐ **Extend:** Help children count all objects on the page up to 20.

Name_____

Let's Count

Listen to your teacher.

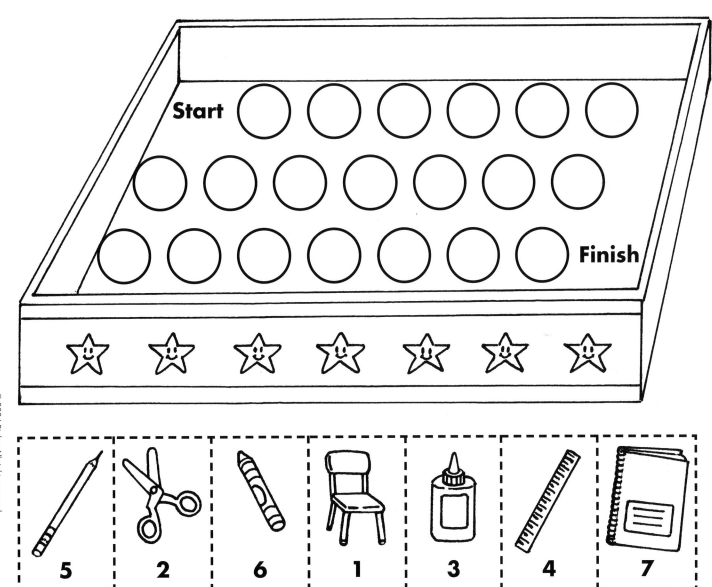

Directions: Cut out the pictures and put them in a bag. Invite children to pick a picture. Help them to name the picture and say the number. Have them count and color that number of circles in the box. Repeat until all of the spaces are colored.

⭐ **Extend:** Invite children to find the objects around the classroom. Have them count the number of items they find.

Name_____

My School Card

Make a school card.

Draw a picture of yourself.

Directions: Invite children to write their name. Help them write their address and phone number. Then have them draw a picture of themselves for their card. Continue the activity by having children ask classmates for their phone numbers.

⭐ **Extend:** Encourage children to draw a picture of their home and write the address.

Name_____

Call Me

Make a telephone.

Call your number.

My Name

My Address

My Phone

Directions: Assist children in cutting and gluing the phone to a sturdy piece of paper. Then help children write their name, address, and telephone number. Have children act out calling their home number.

⭐ **Extend:** Have children ask classmates for their phone numbers and help them to practice calling the numbers on their paper phone.

Name_____

Rooms in My School

Cut out the pictures.

Glue each picture in a room.

Directions: Talk about the pictures as you help children cut them out. Children will glue each picture to the side of the appropriate room. Encourage them to name each room.

⭐ **Extend:** Invite children to share the names of these rooms in their home language and to ask other children what the rooms are called in their home language.

Name_____

Workers at My School

Circle the workers at school.

Write an X through the others.

teacher   custodian   clown

gym teacher   librarian   firefighter

Directions: Talk about the workers shown. Ask children *Is this like a worker you see at school?* Then have children circle pictures of workers who would be at school and draw an X through those who work somewhere else.

⭐ **Extend:** Help children to name people at your school who hold those positions, as they are able.

Name_____

Colors and Shapes

Color. Say. Trace.

blue
□
square

yellow
○
circle

red
△
triangle

green
▭
rectangle

Directions: Help children name and color the shapes at the top of the page. Encourage children to say the color and shape names with you, as they are able. Then ask them to find the shapes in the pictures and trace the shapes in the same colors.

⭐ **Extend:** Encourage children to share with their classmates the names of the colors in their home language.

Name_____

School Days

Cut and glue.

☐	☐
Sunday	**Monday**
☐	☐
Tuesday	**Wednesday**
☐	☐
Thursday	**Friday**

☐

Saturday

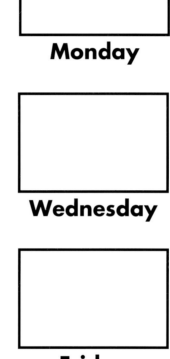

Directions: Ask children to say the names of the days of the week with you. Then have them glue the backpacks on school days and the houses on "home" days. As they are able, encourage children to say *I go to school on _____, I stay home on _____ ,* filling in the blanks with days they go to school or days they stay home.

✸ **Extend:** Invite children to say the days of the week in their home language.

Name_____

What Time Is It?

Listen to your teacher.

Directions: You will need a fastener for this activity. Have children cut out the parts of a clock. Assist them in assembling it. Invite children to put the minute hand on six and the hour hand between eleven and twelve. Say *It's 12:30.* Continue teaching children the time to the half hour in the same manner.

⭐ **Extend:** In pairs, have children set the time to the hour and half hour and ask their partners *What time is it?*

Time to the Half Hour

Name_____

When Does School Start?

Say the time.

Write the time.

_____

It is _____ o'clock.

_____

It is _____ o'clock.

_____

It is _____ .

Directions: Help children say and write the times on the page, as they are able.

⭐ **Extend:** Ask children to tell the times of activities in your classroom, as they are able. Say *What time do we come to school? What time do we eat lunch?*

Name_____

What's Missing?

Cut and paste the pictures.

1 January 	**2**	**3 March**
4	**5**	**6 June**
7	**8 August**	**9 September**
10	**11**	**12 December**

11 November

2 February

10 October

5 May

7 July

4 April

Directions: Have children cut out the pictures. Then ask them to glue the pictures of the missing months where they belong. Encourage children to say the months in order, as they are able to.

⭐ **Extend:** Ask children to name a holiday that they celebrate at home and the month in which it occurs. Children can draw a picture of something they do or eat on the holiday.

Name_____

My Favorite Month

Circle your favorite month.

Draw a picture.

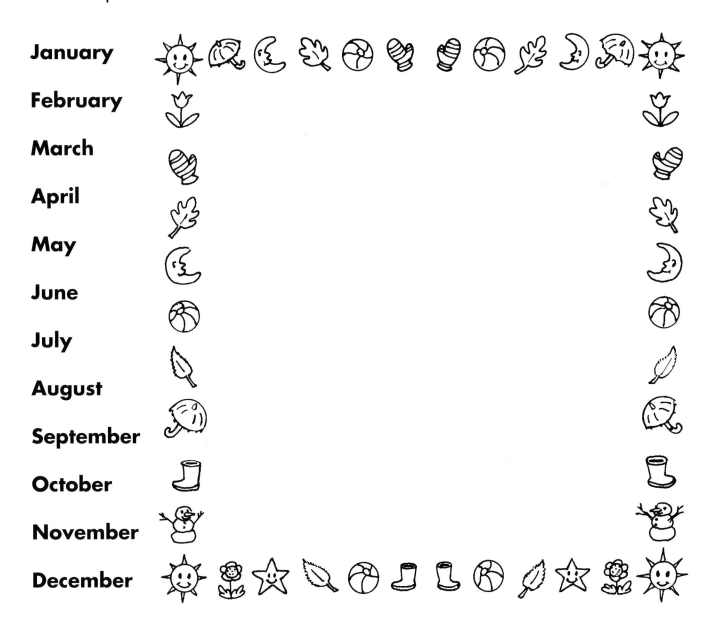

January
February
March
April
May
June
July
August
September
October
November
December

Directions: Have children circle their favorite month. Ask them to draw a picture of an activity they like to do during that month. Invite children to say the months in order, as they are able.

⭐ **Extend:** Ask children when their birthday is. Children can write the month and the day of their birthday, as they are able.

The Bear Family

Match each bear to a chair.

Directions: Tell children each bear family member's name. Then have children cut out each bear. Help them cut a slit in the chairs. Show them how a bear can fit into the slit. Then have them put the correct bear in its chair. Help children to say each bear's name, as they are able.

⭐ **Extend:** Children can draw a picture of their own family.

Name_____

My School Schedule

Draw what you do in the morning and in the afternoon.

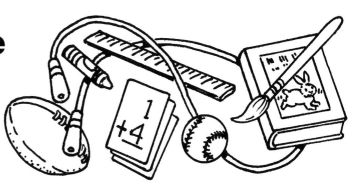

Monday	Tuesday	Wednesday	Thursday	Friday

Directions: Have children draw a picture of two activities per day, one morning activity and one afternoon activity. Help them label the drawings.

⭐ **Extend:** Ask children questions about the schedule, such as *Point to the day you have gym* or *On which day do you have science?* Children may then draw what they do on Saturday and Sunday on a separate piece of paper.

Name_____

Our Busy Classroom

Glue each picture where it belongs.

Directions: Talk with children about activities in different school subjects, such as counting in math and painting in art. Have children cut out the activity pictures and glue them in the appropriate area of the classroom.

⭐ **Extend:** Invite children to talk about their favorite school subject. Ask them about activities they like to do during that learning time.

Happy or Sad?

Look at the picture.

Draw a happy or sad face on Mother Cat.

Directions: Have children look at the scenes. Then have them decide if the mother cat is happy or sad. Point to the pictures above to show *happy* and *sad*. Then ask children to draw happy or sad faces on the mother cat. Encourage children to say *happy* or *sad*, as they are able.

⭐ **Extend:** Invite children to act out how they look when they are happy or sad.

Name_____

What Is Good to Eat?

Find the food. Draw a line.

milk

shoe

chicken

peas and carrots

sandwich

cafeteria tray

juice

ball

apple

hat

notebook

Directions: Talk about each picture. Ask *Is this good to eat?* Then have children draw a line from each food to the tray. Ask children to write an X through the items that they cannot eat. Point to the label and help children say the name of each food.

⭐ **Extend:** Invite children to name some favorite foods that they eat at home. Have them draw a picture of themselves eating that food.

Food

Find the Body Parts

Listen to your teacher.

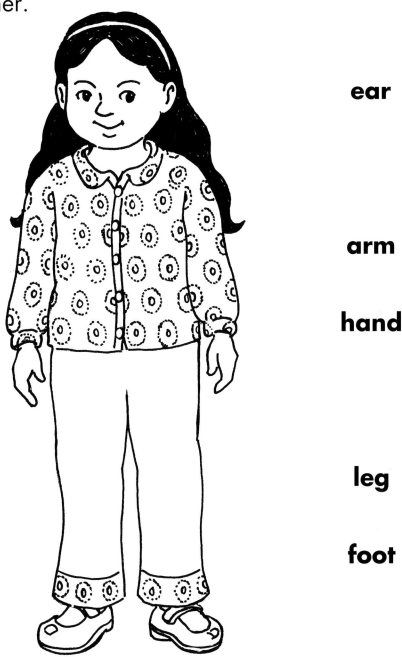

ear

arm

hand

leg

foot

Directions: Ask children to color each body part as it is called out. Continue calling out the body parts until the whole body is colored. Encourage children to say the body parts, as they are able. They can draw a line from the label to the appropriate body part.

⭐ **Extend:** Invite children to name body parts, such as ear, arm, hand, leg, and foot, in their home language.

Name_____

Workers and Tools

What tool does each worker need?

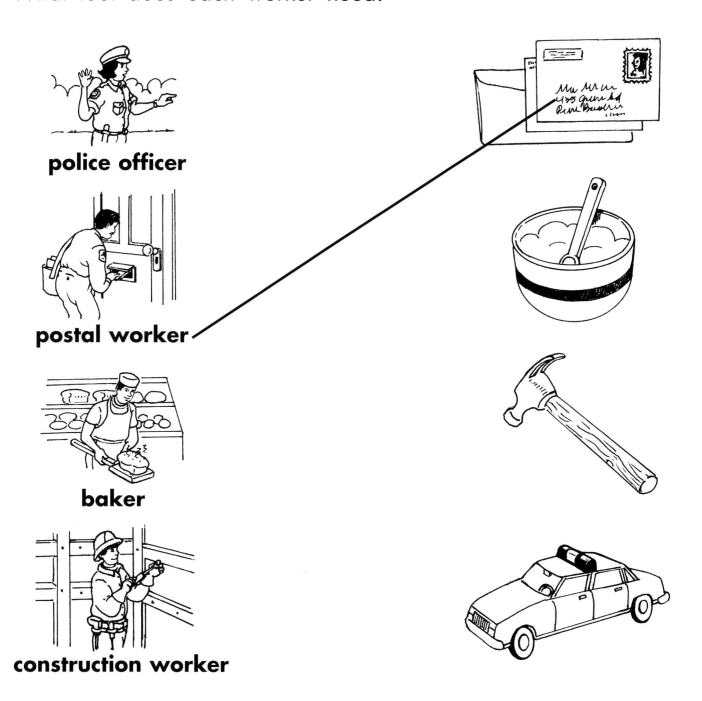

police officer

postal worker

baker

construction worker

Directions: Have children draw a line from each worker to the tool the worker uses. Encourage children to say the name of the occupation with you, as they are able.

⭐ **Extend:** Invite children to think of other jobs and the tools used to do the job. Children can draw a picture of themselves doing a job they would like to do when they grow up.

Name_____

What Letters Are Missing?

Write the missing letters.

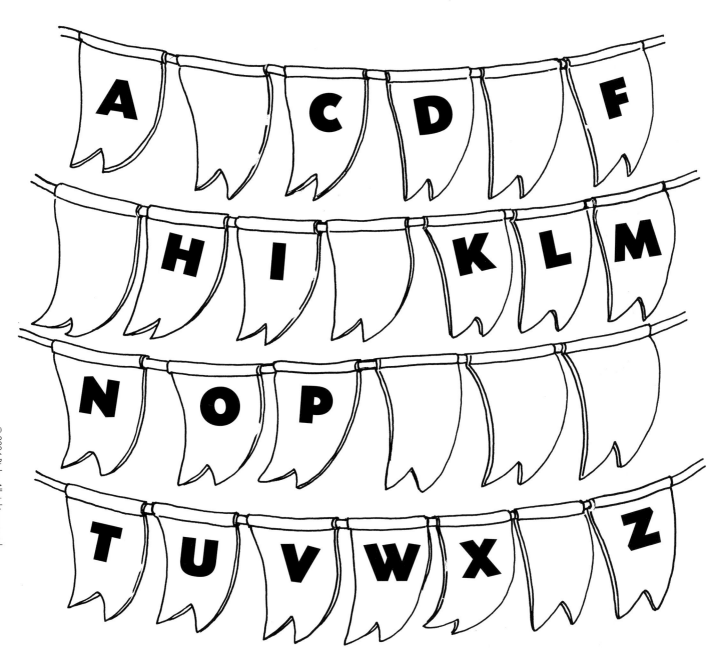

Directions: Have children write the missing letters. Encourage them to say the alphabet.

⭐ **Extend:** Invite children to look for letters around the classroom. Children can write the letters they find.

In the Library

Put each picture where it belongs.

Directions: Have children cut out the pictures and place them in the area of the library where each belongs. Encourage children to say the name of each item, as they are able.

⭐ **Extend:** Children can visit the school library/media center and locate the people, places, and things from the picture.

Handwriting Directions

Writing and Letter Recognition, page 96

Demonstrate the correct way for both left- and right-handed children to place their papers (right-handed—slanted with the lower left corner at the center of the body; left-handed—slanted with the lower right corner pointed to the left of the center of the body). Remind children to sit up straight in a comfortable position with both feet on the floor. Then read the directions with children. Invite them to circle the matching capital and lowercase letters in each group. Then invite them to write letters on a separate sheet of paper. Remind them to hold their pencils correctly. (Have children grasp the pencil between the thumb and index finger above the paint line on the pencil. Have them press the pencil against the middle finger to support the pencil. Ask them to rest the pencil near the large knuckle on the index finger.)

Writing Stick and Circle Letters, page 97

Demonstrate how to use the correct formation to write letters of the alphabet. Remind children that stick letters are made using straight lines. Help children name and then write the stick letters in the first row. Guide children to notice how the capital letter *A* is made with only straight lines, but the lowercase *a* is made from both a circle and a straight line. Point out how the lowercase letters *p, g,* and *q* are "tail" letters—they each have a line that goes below the bottom line. Help children name and then write the remaining letters. Invite children to identify the picture and help them write the word *dog.*

Writing Slant and Curved Letters, page 98

Demonstrate how to use the correct formation to write letters of the alphabet. Point out that each capital letter begins at the top line and touches the bottom line. As you name each letter, encourage children to look for three lowercase letters that touch the top line *(k, h,* and *f).* Remind them that *W* has four slanted lines and to be careful not to make the letter too wide. Help them notice that some capital letters are made with only straight lines, but their lowercase letters have curves. Invite children to write capital and lowercase letters on the lines.

Letter Spacing, page 99

Demonstrate how to write important words. Say each word aloud. Invite children to repeat the word. Point out how each word begins with a capital letter. Guide children to notice the length of each word and the amount of space they have to write it. Remind them to pay attention to the size of each letter and the amount of space between letters. Help children write the words, making sure that all capital letters and the lowercase letters *l* and *d* touch the top line and that spacing between letters is equal. Encourage children to write their first and last names on the bottom line.

Word Spacing, page 100

Demonstrate how to write a message. Read aloud the two sentences that make up this message. Point out the equal spacing between letters and the larger spacing between words. Call children's attention to the two sets of lines. Remind them to begin writing the message on the left side of the lines, continue writing across the page to the right, and then begin at the left side for the next set of lines. Discuss the purpose of a message form with children. Remind them of the importance of writing clearly with equal spacing between words. Read the labels together. Then help children write their own message on the form. Remind them how to use numerals to record the date and the time.

Capitalization and Punctuation, page 101

Demonstrate how to use basic capitalization and punctuation. Discuss each picture with children and read the words next to it. Point out that some of the words are missing capital letters and there are no end marks. Review how to use periods, question marks, and exclamation points. Help children write the sentences on the lines, capitalizing the first word and adding the proper end marks. Remind children to begin writing the sentences at the left side of the page.

Capitalization and Punctuation, page 102

Demonstrate how to use basic capitalization and punctuation. Read the sentences with children. Review use of capital letters for the beginning of sentences and names. Point out the name *Bob* in the first sentence and explain that it needs to begin with a capital *B* even though it is not the first word of the sentence. Also explain that since these sentences tell a story, they can be written one after the other—each one does not need to be on its own line. Remind children about ending the sentences with punctuation marks and then leaving the proper space between sentences. Help them identify the sentences that could end with an exclamation point.

Writing and Letter Recognition

Circle the matching capital and lowercase letters.

1. d b P D

2. o q a Q

3. p g C G   7. n H r h

4. N R m n   8. F L l I t

5. V Y w y   9. c b B R

6. e c E F   10. I M t T I

Directions: Demonstrate for children how to place their papers and hold their pencils. Read the directions with children and invite them to circle the matching capital and lowercase letters in each group. Encourage them to write letters on a separate sheet of paper.

Writing Stick and Circle Letters

Write each stick letter.

T t   L l   I i

Write these stick and circle letters. Then write the word.

A a   B b   C c

P p   G g   Q q

D d   O o   

Directions: Help children name each stick letter and then write each capital and lowercase letter. Follow the same procedure for the stick and circle letters in the other rows. Invite children to name the picture. Help them write the word *dog* below the picture.

Writing Slant and Curved Letters

Write each letter.

K k   V v   W w

X x   Y y   Z z

S s   U u   H h

M m   N n   R r

E e   F f   J j

Directions: As you name each letter, invite children to look for the lowercase letters that touch the top line. Point out that all capital letters touch the top line and that some lowercase letters like *k, h,* and *f* do too. Then encourage children to write each capital and lowercase letter on the lines.

Name_____

Letter Spacing

Write each word. Put space between the letters.

April

Tuesday

Dallas

Maine

Write your first and last names.

_____

- - - - - - - - - - - - - - - - - - - -

_____

Directions: Say each word aloud, and invite children to echo the word. Ask them to write each word, using equal spaces between letters so that each word fits on the lines. Encourage children to write their first and last names on the lines.

Word Spacing

Write the message. Put space between the words.

Berto called. He has a new bike.

_____

- -

_____

_____

- -

_____

Complete the form.

Message
_____
- -

Name: _____   _____

Date: _____   Time: _____

_____

- -

_____

_____

- -

_____

Directions: Read the message aloud. Invite children to copy the message on the lines from left to right. Then explain each part of the form to children. Help them write their own message on the form.

Name_____

Capitalization and Punctuation

Write each sentence. Use capital letters and end marks.

lana can play ball

it is a hot day

look out

can you run fast

Directions: Point to each picture and read the words next to it. Invite children to write the sentences with a capital letter at the beginning of the first word and appropriate end marks.

Name_____

Capitalization and Punctuation

Write the sentences. Add capital letters and end marks.

jan and bob play ball
bob hits the ball
jan catches it
we all play ball

Directions: Read each sentence aloud. Invite children to write each sentence on the lines. Remind them that sentences need to begin with a capital letter and have an end mark.

Handwriting

Answer Key

Unit 1

Page 10: *Things I Do at School*

1. read
2. draw
3. write
4. cut

Page 11: *School Fun*

1. She
2. She
3. He
4. She

Page 12: Ready to Work

Children should match cards that show one book, one pencil, one ruler, and one chair to the table with one child.
Children should match cards that show three books, three pencils, three rulers, and three chairs to the table with three children.

Unit 2

Page 18: *Favorite Colors*

Answers will vary, but children should color the boxes to match the color word and their classmates' favorite colors.

Page 19: *It or They?*

1. It—one house circled
2. It—one cat circled
3. They—two hands circled
4. It—one dog circled
5. They—four girls circled
6. They—two boys circled

Page 20: *Who Is in the Kitchen?*

Mom is smelling the flowers.
Son is eating an apple.
Daughter is reading.
Baby is playing with a rattle.
Dad is making dinner.

Unit 3

Page 26: *Workers in Our Town*

1. is not; is
2. is; is not
3. is; is not

Page 27: *In My Home*

Answers will vary, but pictures and sentences should include items found in the home.

Page 28: *What Did Carmen Do?*

1. third picture
2. fourth picture
3. second picture
4. first picture

Unit 4

Page 36: *What Time Is It?*

1–4. Children should write *It's* on each writing line and read the sentence.

Page 37: *What Is Happening?*

1. raining
2. snowing
3. reading
4. crying

Page 38: *How Big and How Small?*

Pictures will vary, but should match the word meanings.

Unit 5

Page 44: *Animal Puzzles*

Children should match the following pairs:
mice—mouse
geese—goose
fishes—fish
foot—feet

Page 45: *Monkey and Friends*

The picture should be colored with
1. a red bee on the monkey's head;
2. a blue bird in the monkey's hand;
3. a yellow lizard behind the monkey;
4. a green bat next to the monkey;
5. a purple bird under the monkey; and
6. an orange bird on the monkey's foot.

Page 46: *Animal Homes*

1. lives
2. lives
3. live
4. does not live
5. does not live

Unit 6

Page 52: *In the Garden*

1. There are
2. There is
3. There is
4. There are

Page 53: *How Did She Grow?*

Starting at the bottom:
the bottom picture belongs in the bottom box;
the top picture belongs in the second box;
the second picture belongs in the top box; and
the third picture belongs in the third box.

104

Page 54: *I Will Be Big*

The cards should matched to make the following sentences:
A chick will be a chicken.
A puppy will be a dog.
A lamb will be a sheep.
A kitten will be a cat.

Unit 7

Page 60: *Where Are They?*

Children should point to or say the following:
1. in the TV or family room
2. in the bedroom
3. in the kitchen
4. in the bathroom

Page 61: *Things I Do*

Children should write the word *because*
to complete the following sentences:
1. I go to bed because I am tired.
2. I use an umbrella because it is raining.
3. I wear a coat because I am cold.
4. I take a bath because I am dirty.

Page 62: *You Can Do It*

Commands will vary, but should match the card the child is holding.

Unit 8

Page 68: *How Many?*

1. 4
2. 6
3. 2
4. 4

Page 69: *What Do You Do?*

Answers will vary, but should match the partner's responses.

Page 70: *Look Around*

Pictures will vary, but should be of something in the classroom that matches the descriptive word.

On Our Way to English